Melting Glaciers

Melting Glaciers

Richard Edgar Zwez

iUniverse, Inc.
New York Lincoln Shanghai

Melting Glaciers

iUniverse books may be ordered through booksellers or by contacting:

iUniverse
2021 Pine Lake Road, Suite 100
Lincoln, NE 68512
www.iuniverse.com
1-800-Authors (1-800-288-4677)

ISBN: 0-595-33702-3 (pbk)
ISBN: 0-595-66993-X (cloth)

Printed in the United States of America

Contents

Part One

Decline

A melting glacier,
Has a future
Like ice fog.

A melting glacier,
Is a beached whale,
Whose white, soft underbelly
Shrivels under the merciless sun,
And its heart beats ever more slowly,
As its life slips away.

A melting glacier,
Was born ages ago,
And placed its longevity
On the hope of falling snow,
Only to find out that its mass
Cannot compete
With an angry sun.

A melting glacier
Brought its ponderous weight
From lofty mountain peaks
And now its continues its descent
Into our fading memory.

Dripping

Is the glacier's fate sealed,
Such that nothing can be done,
As it melts down?

The puny efforts of humans
Can't succeed.

A phalanx of refrigerators,
Making ice cubes,
Would be like a picket fence,
Holding back the final outcome.

A paltry effort not even makes a dent,
To stop the decline,
As the water drips.

Discovery

What kind of fool
Would buy
A frozen land?

The country was
Rich
In ice and snow.

Now the glaciers melt
And expose
Land.

Loving It

An ice cave
Is the navel of the glacier.

Two lovers gather
To snuggle and sniggle
In their sweet tryst.

A frozen paradise
As warm as reproducing algae.
Within the ice.

They slide like two kids
On a toboggan ride
To where the ice sculptures wait.

Ruling

Whiteness stretches
To the horizon.

Only the highest peaks
Thrust their beaks
To penetrate through
The ice shell.

Coming from the tropics
With their green foliage sea,
I am surprised
That whiteness
Can reign.

Serpent

Kingdoms and rulers
Came and went
But the glacier
Continued to grow
And move.

As an eternal
Cold-blooded snake
Nothing seemed
To stop its movement
Or its life
Until now
With heat enough
To scorch
Its skin.

Surprises

The glacier
is a treasure house.

Disappeared flights,
Forgotten men,
Forgotten thoughts.

All reappear
At the water's edge.

Over With

The sled dogs
Sat on the surface
Of the glacier.

Their ears pricked up,
Their eyes stared,
And they ran away.

The man screamed
At them
And was buried
By an avalanche.

Change of Heart

He loved to whirl around,
His feet
Moved around
Any pole.

But as he
Neared the North Pole
He became more stationary,
As the whirling
Unwound
And became
A mad dash
To his refuge,
Home,
Never to return.

Hope

The glacier looks majestic
Despite its decline.

It's a ribbon of white gold
Among the emerald evergreens.

Its old admirers
Hope that it will regain
Its strength.

The weather may change
In the future
With abundant snowflakes
So that it may regain
Once again
Its vigor.

Fusion

There's a mingling
Of the clouds and the glacier.

Like two lovers
Eager for their embrace
One whiteness
Lies upon the other.

Impressive

It's a massive,
Moving mass.

The glacier
Is a huge magnet
That draws visitors from afar
On foot, skis, crampons,
Planes, helicopters,
And cruise ships.

All seek
Its whiteness,
Its brightness,
Its coolness.

They would like
To drink
Its refreshing water.
Bearing as it does
The taste of centuries,
Of eternity.

Birth

The glacier continues
To be generous.

It still can calve
Huge icebergs.

They glint and glow
Like huge ocean going
Pearls.

They are the product
Of the wondrous
Womb
That gave them
Birth.

Graceful

The glacier melts,
Its waters are
Terribly cold,
Penetrating in the extreme.

Visitors arrive,
They defiantly strip down
To bare
The most skin.

Like of out of place snakes,
They disregard
The cold.

It's time for
A swim.

Eagerness

As the glacier
Continues to move along
Constantly,
It's unstoppable
As the ages
It's been through.

It glides,
It descends,
Deeper in its
Meditation.

It's determined
Like the stirring inspiration
That allows the poet
No rest
Day or night.

Blaze

There were eons ago
A time of fire
And ice.

The glow of the fire
Was mirrored
On the ice.

At the edge
Of the glacier
Is a band of darkness
Once threatening.

Even in a time
Of possible doom
The ice
Moved on.

Strong

The ice remembers
When it was dominant.

Ages ago
It joined forces
With its fellows
To advance together
And cover
Most of the Earth.

The glacier knows
That like the seasons
The tomorrow
Of its might
Is bound
To return.

Beauty

A mistaken notion
Is something apparent.

The ice took over the land
Or did it
Contain the water
So there should
Be land?

The glacier
Doesn't defend its existence,
It has
Its admirers.

Lost

Sleds, snowshoes, crampons
Have left tracks
On the surface
Of the glacier.

Foreigners as well as natives
Allowed their voices
To resound
Against the mountains.

Now all is still,
All is normal,
While the snow eddies
Erase
Everything.

Oneness

The trapper mushed his dogs
Onto the glacier.

He smoked his pipe
As he leaned on
The handles
Of his dog sled.

Snow flurries arose
And smoke and whirling snow
Became one.

Whiteness

The man stumbled in the snowstorm;
He was lost.

He wandered
And wandered
And wondered
And wondered.

Where was he
On the land
Of never ending whiteness
He was as pale
As the surface of the glacier
He melted some of its water
Then moved on.

Notes

The frosty winds
Chase each other.

They are world travelers
Having wandered so much;
Now they are looking
For orifices
In the glacier.

They blow into the holes
And a flute, an ocarina,
A hornpipe, a pan fife
Resound
As in foreign lands
Where oceans lap.

Age

Crevasses appear
Revealing the glacier's age.

Time has worn the
Glacier's
Wind troubled face
For an infinite
Number of years.

What should age
Be to a glacier
Whose birthing
Took thousands of years.

Jewel

Aquamarine
Is the heart
Of the glacier.

Layers of time
Are necessary to create
Such loveliness.

It's not enough to see;
Tue beauty can only
Be found
By coming closer,
Going deeper,
And becoming one
With the ages.

Unheard

The crevasses
Hold many a secret.

Their gaping mouths
Swallow another unwary being:
Another animal,
Another adventurer,
Another sled,
Another plane crash.

Screams rend the frosty air,
But the howling winds,
Care not
And the storm may last
A very long time.

Chilling

Colder than the ice,
Colder still is
The hand of death
Upon the glacier.

The chilling winds
Howl their wails
At another
Misfortune.

But the cold preserves
And will stay the hand
Of corruption
Where nothing turns
To dust.

Eternal

The scientists try to think
Of a name
For an infinite past.

Who knows how long
The glacier has been around
The transparency of the ice
Gives no answer.

Even the distant writings
Of our ancestors
Can't encompass
With ink and pen
Its longevity.

Youth

The winds howl
Over the glacier.

The winds are playful;
They always arise
Anew
With age never
Being a concern.

The winds take the glacier
For granted,
Unappreciative of its existence
Since it is old
And heavy
And massive.

Meltdown

Will the Earth continue
To heat up?

The sun beats down
Unmercifully.

The terns try
Fly away from the
Sun's rays,
The seal looks up
And whimpers,
The polar bear
Can only stick its nose
In the slush.

Part Two

Grandeur

The glacier lies majestic;
That's its nature.

The wilderness
Is its home
And the brilliance
Of the stars
In the arctic sky
Witness to its purity.

The glacier has many visitors,
Not one as enticing
As the Northern lights
That bewitch
All who observe
With the thrilling dance of
The fluorescent seven veils.

Gone

The Vietnamese peddler
Awaits under his conical hat
For his customers.

The youngsters
And some that attempt
To rescue years
Frolic at Malibu
Soon they will seek
Some form of refreshment.

The aging Vietnamese man
Fashioned an ice cream wagon
When he fashioned sides
From abandoned plywood
With his kitchen knife.

He fashioned borders
Out of mahogany strips
His former *acajou*
Of former day has become
His present *bijou*.

As skillfully as Phidias' carvings
Of the frieze at the Parthenon
With his kitchen knife
He carved scenes
Of his native land.

Now he is in America
After having been a soldier
In the Army of the Republic of Vietnam

Alongside with American buddies
Until one day
They melted away.

Fishing

She hoped for a lasting marriage
One in which any problem
Had a solution
Based on mutual love.

She had learned to love a man,
Her father who took her fishing
As his only son.

The days passed and encumbrances
Of past loves and job encounters
Created extra weight
Leading to fissures inclined to weaknesses.

The father needed her daughter's love
And she was gone to help him
It was the tremor needed
So that the cooled mass began to move.

Her husband was gone
Like the filament a fishing line
Slipping in the water
Never to be seen again.

Emptiness

I love not the buildings,
I love their disappearance,
Poetic to me are
The empty spaces
That speak with eloquence
What is no longer.

The concrete path
Leads to an empty area
Devoid of all structures.

Who lived or worked there?
The gray concrete
Doesn't think, doesn't feel, talks not.

Silence is the only voice
Suggestive of what has disappeared.

Empty like the surface of a glacier
Where nothingness
Seems natural.

Flow

He went to college
To get an education
To be his own man.

The semesters
Went on
And on
Forever.

He's gone,
He's
His own man
Floating away.

Ardor

The professor's every move
Is suggestive
To the pretty blonde.

A modern woman
Is a persistent, skillful hunter.

She'll look for him
Until she finds
Where he lives.

She won't be satisfied
Until he satisfies her.

Blazing

The beautiful, silvery airplane
Shines like a
Burning arrow
Inserted
Among the whiteness
Of the clouds.

Down below
A man yearns
For a juicy time
As he waits for its descent
With flaps open.

Fountain

Nature is generous
To keep a man's fountain
Flowing.

Like a hummingbird
That keeps up a beat
In its flight
The flower awaits
Its pollination
To create
A beautiful fruit.

Level

Will my efforts
Stay even?

I didn't rise higher,
I dug deeper.

I polished the stones
To make gems.

Coolness

Both were hip,
Both were cool,
Both were up to date.

Capitalism heard
About it,
To exploit it,
To can it.

They became shaky,
They became dated,
They became passe.

Away

He disliked his job,
It was not challenging.

He didn't like his boss,
He wasn't understanding.

He could have transferred.
Instead he quit.

Now he's desperate,
Searching everywhere,
And even having to move
To another city
Like a boulder
That's loosened
And no one knows
Where it will land.

Progress

The same dull,
Boring job.

He was tired
Of the monotonous routine.

She was employed
Before he quit.

Now his job
Is interesting,
It's taken off,
His thoughts,
His imagination,
His heart palpitations,
Are running wild.

Critical

Pressure increases pressure
To dangerous levels.

Love at a distance
Shrinks the miles.
But not the ardor.

Two people yearn
For each other.

Their imagination
Has a transmitter
That sends signals
Through yearning eyes.

The receiver is the heart
That heats up
To the melting point.

Relentless

At one time
It was parties, movies, shows,
And constant gayety.

The tempo arose
When they really got
To know each other.

Housework, shopping, and paying bills
Sawed away
Creating sawdust
To foul up the timing.

They now wonder
What are singles
Doing now?

Attraction

The ambience
Cannot be disregarded.

There is a setting
For every mood,
Let that never
Be misunderstood.

Robing and disrobing
Are two
Attracting poles
Of searching
Magnets.

Magnets
Turning toward
Each other
Make the current
Flow
Or
Heat up.

Conductors

There are industries
Not included
In the national product.

Love's gears
Turn
Constantly.

There's power there
Not accounted for
On the gauges.

Lovers tend
To merge
And their reticence
Melts.

Impressions

Some people itch
More than others.

Visual, sensory, auditory,
Sensual
Stimulations
Stir every fiber.

The surges
Lead
To urges
That continue to flow
Unceasingly.

Held

She has another man
But she still
Has me.

I recall how
She held me,
How she whispered,
And made promises
Of flowers in spring.

Time has stayed
Frozen in time
Will it ever
Break loose?

Unknown Inside

Who is really
In command?

I toss and turn
Trying to hold back
The fleeting minutes
Of the night
As strong
As wild horses.

If I can't control
My sleep,
Who's in charge?

Questions

Who knows when and if
Dreams come true?

Who are these people
That appear to know something
Or is it nothing?

Who picked
This cast of characters,
Designed their costumes,
Directed their functions,
And brushed on
Their makeup?

Backwards

Do we really
Want to change?

Or do we prefer
To be fossils
Embedded in rock?

Suddenly a river
Comes along
And sweeps layers
And shows us to be
Skeletons.

Permanence

Can I count the treasures
That her heart holds?

Her unappreciated love
Saved me
Driving accumulated shadows,
Specters of the past.

Now everyone realizes
Her value
And others may scheme
To break us up
But now I have
A rock
To cling to.

Present

I'm glad to be alive today,
How about you?

Life can get to be exciting
With beckoning tomorrows,
The constant coquettes
That pull me
Through the night.

Tomorrow may rain or shine
But at least
I got
To see it.

Presence

What makes her stop the talk,
When she walks in?

What makes every head
Turn,
As she throws off eddies
Of stir
And forces throats
To gulp?

She is the embodiment
Of chemistry,
She's a truly devastating compound;
You try to analyze her
But your heart
Only melts.

Tunes

Songs are hangers
For old memories.

There are melodies
We have shared,
They are recordings
Of songs,
To which we've added
Our own words
And feelings.

The eternity of songs
Bring us to our past
But do not return
The loved ones
That shared them
With us.

Food Fooled

It's great to eat something
If it's available.

I, like anyone else,
Like to reach for my wallet
In order to have the good fortune
Of enjoying food
And contributing to
A good cause.

But who can walk
Beyond a cliff?
Alas, within the designated time
I was told all the food
Was gone.

Long Day

It's a very long day
For one who has lost
Everything.

A man is truly poor
Who has been shipwrecked
And marooned
Without
His wife,
His children,
His home.

She promised
For an eternity
To stay the course
And now he faces
The world
Alone.

Charged

Uncle Ted is gone
But he's still remembered.

Aunt Grace gave us
a portrait of Uncle Ted,
who's my wife's kin,
who had a face
like in a horror movie;
How could he had been
Any uglier.

It wasn't my fault
If the car's trunk latch
Smashed down
On his face
And disfigured him.

I

Troubled

It's a shame when people
Think that someone
Can't make a mistake.

The person in question
Has a long, distinguished career
As a government servant,
A crafty politician,
A war hero,
An incisive preacher, or
A shrewd industrialist.

Let him make a mistake
And all his achievements
Take wing.

Trapped

Look out for a fellow
With reddish blue eyes.

His arms are very hairy
Like those of a spider
Just lying in wait
Until you appear
So that he can enjoy
His power.

You won't know
What is disturbing
Until you fall
Within his grasp.

Wonder

Who can tell what else
Is in this life.

Things happen
That are a mystery
Since there may be
No connection
With reality.

There are noises
There are rumbles
Like thunder
Over the horizon.

Safety

She drives down the road
Mindful of the other drivers.

So often you encounter
The speed demon
In the big truck
Used as a tank
That takes chances
And may plow into
An innocent individual
Going to work or
Simply shopping.

Where there is no godliness
No sense of morality
And no civic pride
All is for naught.

Steady

Despite anything that
Goes on in his life
He reports to work.

As mindful as the
Sun that appears daily
To warm and light our days,
The steady worker
Is just as dependable
As he does any task
That he's assigned
Without complaining.

In a society that
Increasingly scorns
Dependability
He shines
Like a beacon.

Remembrances

File away your dreams come true
Nice memories are like
Acquired jewels.

Despite regrets
Despite downfalls
Despite treachery
That might stab
Our hearts
Fond memories
Are a balm.

Who knows
Where we may go
Who we might meet
What could happen
But we continue on.

Armor

A rejection is a miss,
A true shot in the dark.

Conviction can arm
The fiercely loyal
To a cause
And vanquish
The aggressor
Armed with a piecing tongue
That has raised hair and
Bared teeth
Bent on humiliating.

The strong spirit can rise
And shed light
On the truth
And dispel evil.

Illegible

I've forgotten
Her name.

Years have gone,
So many, many,
That have crushed
The bands of my back,
The springs of my knees,
And ransacked the files
Of my mind.

The waves of time
Have obliterated
Her rhyme.

Firm

I never thought
That peace would reign.

I had been so often
At war with this life
Wearing a helmet
That I doubted
That tranquility
Would ever reign.

My qualms
Were gradually eroded
By the steadiness of love
To work away
The accumulated filth.

Assurance

To travel where
You don't know
Where you're going
Requires faith.

You stumble about
As if groping in the dark
Not really knowing where
You're at
And where
It will all end.

Yet despite it all
You find your way
And get the helping hand
Of an angel.

Moistened

Art brings out
Beautiful sensations.

Art gives you an
Appreciation that
Allows you
To touch the rainbow
Through the rain.

Beauty can be reached
And the enriching essence
Drifting onto you,
Like a mist,
Transforms you.

Refuge

A mother's love with its constancy
Can reach a wayward child.

Even when a child acts
With brazen disregard,
With restless yearnings
That lust for power and might,
He can be brought down
From flying near a volcano's edge
Once again
Close to a mother's bosom.

He had been bronzed
And scorched by the sun
Melting away
But he was brought back
To a child's peace.

Free

Wilderness in a being
Can be a strength of soul.

Even a bird
That is made to walk
If only for a short while
Will someday
Be able to fly
Into the heaven
Of its own
Soul.

Creativity is to where
An artist must ascend
If he is to touch
The clouds
And meet the rain
At its origin.

Joined

A bird in a garden
Is a good sign.

Nature is with us
As her creatures stir
As I reach
For my lover
And feel like
Scampering off
With her.

We're like vines
Entwined
Living off
Each other's sap.

Protected

Cries of help call out
Like knife slashes
To the soul.

You rush
Ready to shield
A loved one,
Or even a stranger,
Or bring on
A healing balm.

You're a cloud
Shielding a fellow human
From a hurtful sun.

Yearning

A love that never was
Leaves a gap in the heart.

A love that never developed
Is an ache that arises
Sooner or later
Without fail,
Just like
A lost embryo.

What could have
Happened
Is a mystery
That disturbs
Sleep.

Helpless

A mother's tears
Melt any heart.

To see your own mother
Cry
Is a dissolving, corrosive
Pain
And an embarrassment
Knowing you can't help
Someone so dear.

Years pass and
You still wonder
What you could have done
To alleviate
Your mother's
Tears.

Frozen

A snake is a wonder
To all mankind.

How can something
Walk with no legs
And eat
With no teeth?

Whatever kind a snake
May be
A shiver is felt
And a numbing
Chill.

Instant Decision

Who will turn coward
And run?

People who talk
About what they may do
Have words
Carried in the wind
But when a real danger
Is to be faced
Requiring true character
You have an unknown quantity.

Dangers require
Instant resolution.

Tolerant

Feeling no pain
Is a joy in itself.

Going to sleep
Is a relief,
Yet pain
Can keep you awake
As a thorn
In one's limbs.

Yet the final sleep
Is to be avoided
Even if it means
Suffering endlessly.

Shaky

There are those
Who climb the stairs
Of love.

A love stair means that
You're reaching higher
Stepping on the back
Of a circumstance,
To reach for
An appearance,
A supposition.

In love a stair
Means
Constantly conducting
A trading exchange.

Vapor

It's bad when your home
Bcomes a prison.

A prisoner can develop
A family
Within prison walls
That used to be his home
As his dear ones
Shackled him
To the walls
With bickering chains.

A dream home can disappear
As its essence
Evaporates.

Forsaken

A gift from God
Is a treasure.

Talent comes
Naturally to many
While others, like I,
Have to be content
To touch a piano
But never really play it;
As elusive
As whispering into the wind.

I lost a direction
That I never had.

Lost

To search for something
You can find
Is a known possession.

Will you be led
Down a path
Where there
May be no return
Or come back
Severely wounded?

To grope in the dark
Is misery.

Gone

What has happened
To the town of my youth?

Old buildings
Mean security
To old memories
To keep them
From failing.

Who would have
The cruel heart
To destroy history?

Only

Good love
Like good wine
Only gets better.

How could someone
Coming out of the
Shadows of this life,
A complete stranger once,
Become such a part
Of your life?

She has become
A necessity,
The bones
Of my soul.

Mystery

A youth can
Cause one to wonder.

Children of various ages,
Are a worry,
A concern,
That only grows
Like a storm
On the rise.

Hope that child
Will learn
From experience.

Steel

Is a child's head hard
Because its young?

Why can't a child
Listen
With such good hearing?

Advice
Like mortality
A child
Can disregard.

Inevitable

Simple things
Are hard to control.

Who can dominate
Something simple
As a pimple
Or a volcano?

You suffer dearly
When a little something
Leaves
No hope.

Explosion

Urges come
In surges.

Like a tidal wave
Arising from
The bottom of the sea
An urge may burst out,
Suddenly.

An enormous wave
Can devastate
A whole country.

Vanished

Is a model
A model woman?

A model is a sprite
Is a spirit
And you could
Be disappointed
Trying to capture it.

She is a vision
That disappears.

Fatal

To chugalug a love
Is to seek drowning.

Let love
Come gradually
Like the extending shadow
Of a cloud.

Loving too soon
Can be too intoxicating
Too deadly.

Maybe

Being a parent
Can be so strange.

Children can cast
A parent into the sea,
Yet others look for
A parent
Who's disappeared,
Who they have never known
Who has left
Without a trace.

Children like all humans
Are unpredictable.

Crushed

Why should we be afraid
Of an inspection?

An inspection
Sends seismic waves
Throughout our human frame
And creates tidal waves
In a person's stomach.

If they don't like
What you have
You only die once.

Unstable

Everyone dreams of having
An island.

Reality is cruel
In its demands for water and food
Of electricity
Of civilized fun
Where there's only sea water
Elevated coconuts
Lightening storms
And the relentless moans of the ocean.

A dream,
Like fog,
Can fade when the sun comes out.

Unknown

She left us
A pretty portrait.

I look at her
With her long, auburn hair,
Bright eyes,
Clean skin,
And rosy lips.

She's my ancestor
But that's all
I know.

Thoughtful

He had a memory
Like a recorder.

He could remember
All sorts of information
About all kinds of things
But with a tender heart
Knowing you personally
What he could do for you
And when.
He was truly a beam of sunlight
In a person's life.

Somebody notices you
And also has
A ready smile.

Available

She's a compact
Beauty.

She's lovely
In a small package
Brief and to the point
Not like a model
Long like stretch limousine.

She's all a man could want
Within easy reach.

Fake

They named her Helen
For a reason.

She didn't come from Troy
But likes horses
All the same
She doesn't ride them,
She doesn't breed them,
She doesn't groom them,
They might as well be
A cardboard prop
So she can pose
With them.

She'll stand by the horses
And has her photograph
Taken,
Smiling.

Safe

Nothing can be kinder
Than a welcoming bed.

To tuck oneself
Under nice, clean sheets
Laundered by my lady love
Is being a husky
Lying warmly
In a snow bank
Insulated by the snow.

To lie in peace
In the stillness of the night
Is a blessing.

Civilized

A tree is a sign
Of true civilization.

To live in a city
Were trees
Are considered a hindrance
Is a place
Trying to be
A desert.

Thinking will change
But at what a price?

Contained

Versification can be
A playground.

Poetry exalts
The child in all,
The sense of wonderment,
The excitement of the find,
And the drama of living.

Words are the cups
Of a poem.

Enduring

Create a myth
For elevation.

A life
That twists and turns
Like a pebble
In a wave
Come out
Even more
Polished.

Capture the transient
Bubbles of the seashore.

Transient

I had love
Within my grasp.

Should I list
Someone's wrongs or
Their defects
Like spots on
A caterpillar?

It was an incredible time
But didn't last.

Exaltation

Everyone blames another
For destruction.

Destruction is ugly
But not really;
Like a butterfly bursting
Its jewel-like chrysalis
It's a foundation
For a brighter tomorrow.

Wipe your forehead,
And recreate even better.

Sleight

Fake smoke and
Fake lives.

A theater creates
Fakery to reveal reality
With make believe fog
Mimicking a cloud.

A familiar shadow
Of nothing.

Uncertain

A hollow
Is waiting.

An opening can
Lead to discovery
Or is it a trap
Deep within a cave
As you might look
Into the well of a heart.

Not even exploration
Might reveal the unknown.

Paralyzed

A worried mind
Creates its nightmares.

Like dark silhouettes
Against a light background
Our daylight nightmares
Parade.

To be stuck in indecision
Shows no exit.

Pathways

A name
May reveal much.

His name was Nelson
Although he'd never
Been to sea
Like earth
That's never been
Sediment.

Who knows what
We might have been.

Incredible

It was only a
Papier-mache head.

Long after the theater
Had ceased to exist
A prop head
Brings back memories
Slipping off the stage
Of life.

A prickly feeling
Can bring back a memory.

Fragments

A photograph
Is worth a thousand feelings.

The postcard
Is an exotic backdrop
To our trip
Although we no longer
Touch the sand,
Feel the breeze,
Or slosh the water
It's enough.

A record
Can only be partial.

Good

I kneel on the front step
Of her altar.

If feel her presence,
Her breath,
Her stare
But I've never
Ever spoken to her.

A feeling lasts
Even if it's not real.

Hurt

She's not what
I expected.

She was built
To stir desire,
To create wants,
To demand satisfaction

Since I fist saw her,
She's only caused
Me pain and despair

Continuing

She can express herself well
With her body.

Only a gesture was needed
To stir the dusty leaves
Of my soul
And they've never
Stopped turning.

A constant stirring
Is like the waves of the sea.

Ashes

Applause
Is short lived.

No matter
How they try
Fame is
For a moment.

Men try so hard
To keep the flames
Of fame burning bright.

Earthbound

He tried to explain
The Big Bang.

He tried to raise
The curtain of my ignorance
By attempting to explain
A theory
That's only a tunic
Covering his meager facts.

Science flaps its wings
To create a stir.

Concise

Peeks are better
Than staring.

You can distill
The essence
Of something
In a peek.

Tell me the story
In a synopsis.

Tenderness

More happens
Offstage.

An wisp of recognition
Is all I asked of her
She closed my lips
With a kiss
And I believed.

There is authority
In affection.

Preserved

An extended belief
Is difficult.

I couldn't erase
The thoughts of her
That still gushed
In the fountain
Of my being.

She lasts
And lasts.

Lasting

Lovers fear the lasting lashes
Of the gods of love.

There's the immortality
Of failed loves
And jealousy
Of what are
Now mere phantoms
Of yesterday

Passing remembrances
Still create stings.

Clarify

Brighten my hopes
So we can see
That I have a future.

Don't tell me
What it should be
That's like the flamingos
To hold up
My dreams.

Dry offerings
Are stale toast.

Meanings

She looked at me,
Strangely.

Does she seek
To plumb the depths
Of my soul
And to test
How profound
Are my feelings?

Will she see
Clearly?

Understandable

My eyes showed
My supplication.

Even at a young age
On can be suppliant
At the feet of a lady
That tosses her head
And looks away.

My Helen,
You're still in Troy.

Hooked

Things can happen
Underground.

Deceit, regret,
Betrayal
Are fishhooks
Hard to retrieve.

I took the bait,
And I'm still caught.

Heights

Her wings
Reached for elevation.

Her wings
Got mistaken
With the clouds
At that great height.

If she's a goddess,
She'll return to her realm.

Stillness

She's gone,
And I'm shocked.

My former student died
In the deepest poverty
Living in a car,
Begging for food,
Of an infected C section,
And I didn't know
Anything about her situation
Until I was told
That her spirit had migrated.
Where I can no longer reach her;
Death provided for her
What life didn't,
Peace.

Never underestimate
Human kindness.

Flight

What if he had been
My brother?

If he had been my brother
Would his presence,
His words,
His thoughts,
His clarity of thinking,
His foolishness
Have changed
My life?

Possibilities
Are just butterflies.

Question

Throw seeds
To see
What will grow.

My friend
Has plants with no name
And with unknown
Origins.

Man searches
For the unknown
And expects a surprise.

Learn This

If you're strict
You won't be loved.

Fairness and firmness
Go together,
Freedom for all to do
As they please
Leads ultimately to chaos
Like a sputtering candle
That has lost its purpose
To steadily shine.

The ship lost its
Rudder.

Sickness

Any dust
Can make you sneeze.

She and her husband
Loved wealth
But silver and gold dust
In large amounts
Gave them
Pneumonia.

The road to wealth
Can be disabling.

Sweet

Everybody likes
A smiling baby.

A baby shines
On everyone
Like a sunbeam
Of delight
Transfiguring
All.

A baby simple joy
Lingers.

Riches

The orange sun
Looks good enough
To eat.

Poetry lets us pick
The cotton
Of the clouds.

A gunny sack
Full of poetry
Is a treasure.

Bower

I gave her a
Poem as a flower.

Violets, jasmine,
Honeysuckle,
And red roses
form a garland
Of verses.

A wreath of poems
Competes with a garden.

Paths

Change is in
The minds and hearts.

The teenager said
That she'd grow out of it,
The adult declared
That he'd change his ways;
What is needed
Is the moving of a boulder
By rushing water
Or an earthquake.

Sediments speak to us
In foreign tongues
That change took place;
But at what cost?

Art

Wise is the man
Who listens to his love.

The waves of the sea
Change the patterns
Of the sand
As a sculptor
Takes his time,
Chip by chip,
As a lover alters
His love
Kiss by kiss.

Love's chisels
Are tender nibbles.

Enticed

Variety is our hope
For change.

The smells of various lands,
Cilantro, cumin, cinnamon,
Chili, rosemary, sage
All invite taste
As a lover
With the promise
Of greater sensations.

Letting yourself go
Allows freedom
For growth.

Vision

Who can erase
A deep impression?

She appeared
As the moon coming
From behind the clouds,
Like a rainbow
Among dark rain clouds,
To light my life
So that love's beams
Might once again,
Penetrate.

A love one
Is needed
To lighten
Your load.

Creation

Tradition is a weight
That sinks.

Repetition for centuries
Allows for a boring routine
The proportions thought
To be perfect
The style reduced to a rite
That groans with boredom
Against a nature that seeks
Always to alter
So as to form additional beauty.

Let the wind and the water
Teach us about changing patterns.

Toughness

A challenge is a clarion call
To bring out another facet.

The diamond is not churlish
In giving up its light;
The dash of the sparks
Are in a hardness
That doesn't disdain
Elegance.

Diamonds are forever;
They are built that way.

Real

Poetry can be
A balm
To a hurting spirit.

The poet does not hide
In the ivory tower,
He searches out
The pain and the joy
Of every man
And seeks to soothe
And heal
The broken body
And the melted heart.

Verses are
Generous pelicans.

Thespian

Rodents are not beautiful
But they stick around.

A mouse is a creature
With a sense of timing
As he plans his appearance
To create
A devastating effect.

Poor mouse, its talents
Are not appreciated.

Enigma

Why get married
To complain?

A marriage can last
So long
That it should
Have a large trunk
And deep roots
As well as fine hardwood
Yet it can break
When a lightning strikes.

A splinter
Has unpredictable
Jagged edges.

Siren

She sings
And moistens the notes.

She kisses the mike
And music reeks
Of romance
Reserved
For every
Listener.

She stops singing
And seeks
The most affected.

Why?

When is a monster
A monster?

An elephant
Is covered with wrinkles,
Has a tremendous snout,
Tusks like sabers,
Huge weight and bulk,
And is still
Worthy of admiration.

Some things are hard
To understand.

Misunderstood

How could it be
Autobiographical?

I shook my wand
And a sprite appeared
Clad in sparkles
And nimble of toe
Spreading a cape
To glide
About my chamber.

Would I like
To be a fairy?

Desire

Everyone wants
To see an alien.

With all the
Wonders of nature
And the majesty of space,
The imagination
Remains restless,
Unsatisfied,
Hungry
For more.

Man is
Never satisfied.

Fractured

A mother's dismayed look
Is an open book.

Nothing can crack
The surface of the Earth
Like the strife
Caused by the spirit
Of a willful child.

With a tough child
A parent can
Climb high walls.

Wasteful

They disdained literature
And produced a desert.

A country where poets
Are held in low esteem
And ignored
Is a land
Where verses
Are minerals
Of value
Cast aside.

Poems are used by some
To cushion glassware.

Light

Carols bring back
The full joy of Christmas.

Even in the Southern states
People can dream of snow
While not worrying
About shoveling
And about reindeer
Without looking
After them.

Dreams are lovely
And free.

Happiness

Babies of all lands
Are pretty.

A new born calf
Is a delight to the heart
So sweet, so gentle
Unlike a few years later
A bull
Ready to impale you
With its horns.

Ready
for a continuing joy.

Classified

Everyone ends
Up being scored.

The love
That's freely given,
The good intentions,
The willingness
To help
Are scored
By the unwilling.

We hope
To score high.

Decision

What can I do
With him?

That fellow
Means trouble;
He's a boulder
That can't be
Dug out.

Don't complain;
Help the fellow.

Disappearing

She's definitely
On fire.

She's aflame:
Her eyes,
Her limbs,
Her walk,
Show
That she's burning.

How close
Can you get
To her?

Flash

We're lovers
Of speed.

Lightning
And tornado
Are our symbols
When we fall
In love
With a flying start.

Slow progress
Can be so boring.

Wealthy

We're increasingly
Upscale.

Wood and stone
Were good enough
For our ancestors
Then we fell in love
With gold and silver
But now white gold
And platinum
Are our new loves.

Let's get uptown.

Discardable

So who wants
To be puny?

Let me be a phoenix
Let me rise
From the ashes
Of my aging body
Through science's marvels.

Let my old bottle
Of a body
Be a throwaway.

Renewal

Let me return
As a starfish.

The sea air is a tonic,
The sea waves are a massage,
The sand is heat therapy,
To my tire body
As it requests ardently
To become part
Of the sea scene
Indefinitely.

Let me stay at the beach
Forevermore.

Arrows

Missiles are launched
Every day.

Words slung
Like deadly missiles
Sting the loving breast.

Soothing words
Are a balm.

Charms

There's smoothness
Everywhere.

The silk of a baby's head,
The softness of a lady's arms,
The handshake of a gentleman
Are poems of human blessedness.

May she always repose
By my side.

Unknown

She loved me
Without details.

A splendid love
Is one that rolls on
With no bumps
On the road
And no
Flat tires.

She kept right on
Going.

Reflections

Sheen and color
Melt eyes.

Satin enclosed her
As it revealed shadows
Enhancing
Light reflected
By her curves.

A lovely
Swelling sea.

Loss

As his life
Slipped away.

I cradled him in my arms
The wetness revealing
His essence flowing out,
Away,
Irreplaceable
That no angry incantation
Could contain.

His eyes
Grew dim.

Heavyweight

Check your bank account
Before you love her.

She had him figured out
To be her Fort Knox
So she didn't have to sweat
Trying to find gold
And maybe coming out
Empty.

It didn't matter if
He ended up penniless.

Disreputable

They're mighty flighty
With your money.

They get sore
If it's their money
But they send your Washington
To Valley Forge.

Your funds have now crossed
The Delaware.

Inspiration

Beware of a
Hidden force.

What compels me
Once again
To take down my lyre,
Run down the hills,
And scamper
On the meadows
Of Arcadia?

Poetry seized
Me and made
Me frisky.

Again

Forgive me,
Please.

A friend forgives
Our thoughtlessness,
Our drifting away,
Our neglect,
Our disappearance,
Until invisible ties
Draw us near once more.

I've not
Forgotten you.

Unappreciated

Let me find
My way.

Allow me
To search again
Through the dusty attic
Of my inspiration
For a jewel
I should have treasured.

We neglect
So much.

Acting Career

He won
First prize.

He was at the height of popularity
In his school
He could fold a new teacher
Into quartos
And didn't know
Shakespeare.

Hope he gets a job
As a standup comedian.

Compensation

She gave all she had
To give.

She's did all she could
Both to make me happy
And miserable
Now I see her
As both sun
And rain.

What else did
She have in store?

Man Insect

He's a lover
Of bricks and lumber.

Building is in his blood
To erect houses
Or do remodeling
So that you know
He's been there.

He was bit by ants
When he was a child.

Slow

Never call him
A slacker.

He will get to his work
Just give him
Enough time
To start
He's like the giant earthquake
That will strike California
Someday.

He's been looking
For the starting line.

Trapped

I'll never have
A business place.

I could be a jail cell
Although it occupies
A whole building;
My merchandise
Would confine me in
And make me a slave
Of its care.

Let me stay free.

Waterfall

Opulence
Is a treasure chest.

India never gave me
The shovels full
Of diamonds,
Emeralds,
Or rubies
I yearned for.

Let me bathe
In a jewel waterfall.

Release

Fill my house
With laughs.

Come, my friends,
And join me
And with laughter
Drive away any care
That still lingers
In the corners
Of my home.

Laughter sweeps.

Hurry

Tell me,
Please.

If you have
Something to say
Out with it
Or I may never
Get to hear it
As the hour is late
By life's
Stingy clock.

We have
Only now.

Changing

What would
You suggest?

Should I call
To beg you
to forgive me
even if I hate
myself
for doing it?

Such a pain.

Found

He'd make
The perfect stranger.

You bump into him
You smile at him,
He smiles back,
You've never seen
him before.

Who is
this person?

Freed

Poor choice.

She was always was
Undependable,
She proved
Unreliable,
She had
No self-discipline,
And she let me go.

Thank you.

Expressive

If you would
Tell us.

If there is a
Grievance in your heart
Let's play a guitar
And sing
And while the music
Is fresh in our ears
Confess your pain.

Release us.

Pitchers

Even now
we're throwing.

We're no longer cavemen
Throwing rocks
Yet we still throw balls
Or hand grenades and
Occasionally we throw
A fit.

He's the strong right arm
of his boss.

And Then?

I stay awake
Wondering.

Making decisions
Are one of the biggest pains
Of life
Since we mostly
Throw dice
As we gamble
With fate.

I hope that the dice
Are not loaded.

Sparkle

Deeper and deeper.

Lasting and deepening
Is our friendship
As we share
A moment
There's the glint
Of diamond.

Flash.

Lost

The fondest words
Are not said.

What I thought
Had no value,
Had my tongue dried,
Or my willingness
Evaporated?

Wasted in transport.

Fleeting

It only went
Higher.

My voice grew
In a futile attempt
To hold together
What no longer
Made any sense.

Gritting my teeth.

Changing

Changes must come.

With no changes
There'd be
No newspapers;
Be they good or bad
We like to have news.

We married
And it changed
Both of us.

Fate

The lone
Survivor.

The little catfish
Last of my fish
In the aquarium
Swam in the stream
Where I release it;
May God bless it
And protect it.

Good bye, little friend.

Together

The big fellow
And his little friend.

We lived by contrasts
And never stuck
Together;
Let's get along
As life
Hurries by.

Hug me,
Please.

Powerful

I'm sorry
But I must write on.

It's a whirling
Mental machine
That I know it's useless
To stop
With the only result
Being scraped knuckles.

Like life
Writing continues on.

Torrid

It's a pull
Like an undertow.

I continued to look at her,
I tried to disguise it
But she caught on
And didn't stick her nose
In the air
Even though I had to sneak
Another look at her
As I resisted but
Her every part
Spoke poetry to me.

There was not a rock around
To cling to, to stop me from
Being hauled off by the current.

Barbed

Not only ice
Melts.

He swung a whip
Like barbed wire
Out of meanness
Bubbling caustic material
From goodness knows
What irrational
Fountain.

He scoured my back
Like a glacier.

Slippery

I didn't take much
To get her angry.

I spoke to another woman
About my trouble,
But she said I should have been
To her to ask her
To help me.

I guess I'll never
Get back.

Uncertain

Will he
Or will he not?

He said that he wanted
To come
But like a prediction of rain
He added
That he would do it
If nothing else came up.

What do I
Really have?

Hidden

The colors
Are important.

She believes in
Buried treasure;
She buys clothes
She doesn't wear
And books
She never reads.

She must be
Part mole.

Sharp

Where does
He sharpen it?

He believes in cutting words
Like saw blades,
Like the leaves of cactus plants,
Like the fins of fish,
Like a lightning slicing clouds
To tear me up
Because of hate
Or love.

I have to put myself
Back together.

Sales

But will
It sell?

Money drives
Many a writer,
An agent,
An editor,
A publisher.

Write a cliché
Or not all—
What advice!

Surprise

Poor doctor,
He fainted.

The physician
Drew my blood
But only found
Printer's ink.

Is it a miracle?

Sorry

I threw a hook
And it caught it.

I've fished
In many waters
And caught
Pretty fish
And some
With ugly shirts.

If I throw out this hook
I might catch a shark.

Evil

He moved
In pain.

He shuffled
On his knees
To which
Were attached
Barbed cactus
In order to please
His god.

Why do some people
Have mean ancestors?

Faces

My old student
Ran to see me.

Years had passed
And time had gone along,
Yet my student
Hadn't forgotten me
And recognized my face
Since he felt that I hadn't changed,
But I couldn't believe that.

The eyes of love
Are kind.

On

It continues.

I'm on a writing jag
That carries me along,
Headlong.

When it will it stop?

Clash

Where can bickering
Take you?

We argued
Much too much
And eventually
Argued
With hatred.

A rolling stone
Can roll backwards.

Restless

I tried
To sleep late.

I fool myself
By trying to stay in bed;
I hope endlessly
To regain sleep
But I wake up
And then I hate myself
Since I must be
Like a pelican thinking
In a hurricane.

:Let me turn over
and start again.

Faithful

Others left
But not her.

She lives with me
After all that goes on;
I try to be generous,
And work,
And work,
And work at it.

Like life,
She's still here.

Lines

Why did
I ever start?

Be it sentences
Or verses
My hand may wear off
But not my inspiration.

It's a star;
Not just any light.

Bursting

Is it time
To flee?

The door of
Imagination
Is about to burst
Sweeping aside
All considerations,
All festivities,
All plans.

The tug
Is too great.

Hidden

Why wear a mask?

He shows gruffness,
He snarls,
He sulks,
He disapproves,
He shoves aside,
But can't completely hide
His genuine warmth.

Why hold it in?

Guidance

Where will the
The young ones go?

While in class
I guided you
Like little yellow goslings
Trying to cross
The street.

Once gone
I hope to see you
And hear good tidings.

Return

Is he really gone?

Will a writer
Continue in his
Unproductive stage
Creating in his heart
Deep anguish
While lying next to his muse
And feeling her warmth?

He already
Feels a surge.

Found

Surely they can find
Their way.

Are professors
And writers
Gone to
Their netherworld
Among the storms,
The stars,
And the suns
And forget
To return home?

What's fond and comforting
Deals with the pole star.

Astonished

A poor excuse
Has winged feet.

I asked myself
Why
She hadn't written
Anything
She said
That she needed
Find her pen
As if one missing star
Would darken the night.

If she can lie so sweetly
Can I trust myself
Not to believe?

Changing

Change comes often
Without permission.

She likes to think
Of herself as being
Cosmopolitan and metropolitan
By the elegance
Of her clothes
And remaining unapproachable,
But would a flower
Grow an unfolding bud?

Could a human being
Never change
And allow snobbery
To replace loneliness?

Famous

Is fame
Priceless?

Fame allowed
Him to enjoy at no cost
The wind and the stars
At the beach
On a political junket,
As well as
The many receptions,
Gobs of grub,
Gangs of festivities,
Garnishments at social clubs;
Not to mention
Ribbon cutting events.

Just being there
Would have been enough
For him.

Flutter

Butterflies follow the dart
Of their hunger.

Carelessness and confusion
As well as craziness
May do the work
Of more methodic approaches
Just as a pruned hedge
Withstands the clipping
In order to achieve order
And symmetry.

He became lost
In order to be found.

Bronze

He was as rigid
As a statue.

He was a living fossil
Petrified in stone
With rigid rules
And regulations
That allowed no
Fresh air to filter in,
So "Inflexible"
Became his nickname
And part of his
Fossil record.

He was a goon
Posing as an administrator.

Dangerous

He became a kamikaze
Late in life.

He crawled on the land
Munching his way across
Guided by nothing but
His appetites,
His thoughts,
And his memories
So that to the motorists curses,
In his old age,
Meant nothing
As he remained oblivious
To his surroundings
As the concrete
On the highway.

He was
A solid, stolid citizen.

Prickly

Who would like
Work with evil men?

History seem to demand
Thorns along with its roses
As notoriety
Is exchanged for
At a higher price
Than talent.

Are they flesh
Of a different kind?

Rich

Her purse was
Chock full.

Quaint were her ways
Picked up
On this or that Riviera
Holding her nose
At events in her home town
While the barbarians
In the hinterlands
Work at Dad 's factory.

Her roots had spread
Horizontally.

Mighty

Horrible thoughts
Cloud the mind.

If I became
The Big Cheese
And was
The Big Stinker
Would I turn
Ruthless?

Could I ride
The skeleton horse
of Death?

Jaded

Tedious was
Favorite word.

Tired of
Anything and everything
The hallmark
Of one who went
Through life's delights
Quickly
As if he had puffed
On life's cigar
And now had nothing
But ashes.

He drew the word "bored"
On the ashes.

Genteel

The old gal
Knows some stuff.

A long-gone era
Claims her,
She knows what's
Tulle and taffeta
And crepe de chene;
Now in an age
Of blue jeans
She flutters
Like a butterfly
With iridescent wings.

Can elegance
Ever be out of style?

Crumbling

He's a rejection
Machine.

Quite an editor
They have,
He returns fiction
As if he was
Playing tennis;
If you're not
A writer of note
Then you're just
A chimera
Of English literature.

A individual
Who prides himself
Of being tough.

Outcast

Who is she?

She came
Out of nowhere,
A blot to refined people
Who think
She does not belong in society:
A parvenu, an upstart,
An ostrich among swans.

But she sure
Has style.

Luminary

She's a brilliant
Newcomer.

She brandishes
Her nom de plume,
Lilting all along,
Lillian Lilly,
Was taken up
In a gush,
Like a geyser,
By romance novel
Aficionados.

I long
For her love letters.

Learned

A true scholar.

A fine English professor,
A searcher
Of grammatical bacteria,
Of punctuation microbes,
A terror
To unschooled, uninitiated
Technicians
Who fell
Under his magnifying glass.

Perfection
Is no hyperbole.

Forgotten

Darkness
Filled the Earth.

Obscurity
Can cloud a mind
Devoid of luminaries
As I searched
For a remembrance
His face faded
Into the past.

Piecemeal recollections
Are the crossword puzzle
Of the mind.

True

She's refined.

A creature
Created by Beauty herself,
She scornfully rejects
Unpolished suitors
Who would shadow
Her violets.

He didn't
Have a chance.

Endless

He'll talk to himself
If need be.

A friend that shuffles reminiscences
Like playing cards
Is a threat
To polite society.

Would that
He'd burn himself.

Lucky

She believed in change
And her ability to control it.

She had sharpened
Her claws
By preying on men
And discarding them;
She only gave me a scratch
But the fever from it
Melted my ardor.

I was going into the pit
But the sharp edge
Melted my ardor.

Incomplete

I needed her,
And I'm not ashamed
Of it.

When she's gone
The house is empty
My heart is vacant
My being is hollow.

When she returns
It's a party.

Fresh

A child's actions
Are a novelty.

Cowboy boots
Led my children's dreams;
I considered them no less
Than those of an adult
As I treasured
Their blossoming intelligence.

A child's open mind
Is a discovery.

Treasure

A practical wife
Is money in the bank.

A wise wife
Is a shipwright
That takes care
That caulks for any leak
And keeps
Her home afloat.

Frugality is
A marriage's hope.

Classifications

He never knew
What should be
His nickname.

Urbane and sophisticated
He considered himself;
He had pigeonholed
Many a human creature
Without hesitation
Given them tags and labels
From elderly matrons
To little kids
Much like
A zoologist.

Some exasperating
Individuals
Are hard to take.

Coward

Treachery is a sin.

To throw a rock
And hide your arm
Is despicable;
He used his underling
To fire his employee.

Villainy lurk
In the shadows.

Unavoidable

I couldn't stand
The itch any longer.

I had to write a poem
Can a mother stop
Having birth
When the time has come?

The poem was mature
And ready to be delivered.

Lucky

A bird will
Repeat its song.

I am fortunate
To repeat my song
Goodness knows
When it comes time
To sing.

A song is the embodiment
Of one's soul.

Goodies

The world is gone to sea
In chips.

Munching has taken
The place of drinking
Every one wants to be
An old salt.

Raise the level of the ocean
In your veins.

Phantoms

Let's only die
For a moment.

Halloween has come again
And the living dead
Appear
In a parody of death.

I'd love to scare Death
To death.

Realization

Is what we ridiculed
Bound to be our destiny?

Certainly what comes along
Might have been laughable
At one time
But destiny is a
Purveyor of bubbles
That could become
Iridescent in the sunlight
Or just plain transparent.

Is there a day
That couldn't bring
Unpredictable weather?

Changing

It's hard to
Keep it straight.

A story
Can change
so much:
first it's liquid,
then it's gas,
next it might
just appear
as a solid.

The originator
Would not recognize
His own story.

Unchanging

Every day
Should be a joy.

We should be grateful
For what each day will bring;
A blessing
To just have seen it
And experience its offerings
Be they expected
Or surprises
Yet glad
To be around.

There are bound to be
Twists and turns
On the road of life.

Wild

It's help the economy;
Stupid.

There are lots of races
Going on
Dealing with
Recently arrived
Credit card
As every man and woman
Dashes to the stores
To burn up
The new buying power.

King Midas
Didn't know about plastic.

Heat

They've already
Been to Hell.

Lots of smiles
Were exchanged
When dealing
With the firm's future
But the worker's
Who saw all those
Well-dressed executives
Arriving and leaving
Didn't know
That in their briefcases
They carried red-hot pokers
For the laborers.

Have no hope
When you enter.

Blaze

Every little light
Can shine.

A torch here,
A torch there,
Is a string
of lights
of those that
seek to illuminate
their path
to the future.

One day
All of the torches
Will combine.

Amazing

Oh, the wonders
Of the modern age.

The intended construction
Of the interstates
On which the motorists
Would take flight
And sail the highways
Like a man-o-war
On the winds
Has ground down
To gridlock.

The road
Was like a stalled
Weather front.

Blinded

Not a light
In the East.

In the land
Of fluorescent lightning
As in the interior
Of a cave
The office worker toils
To hold back
The roiling flood
Of paperwork.

Plodding thoughts
Are the snowdrifts
Of reports.

Sucked

It's as sure
As sin.

A barricade
Of holy books
Tumbles down
After being undermined
By our desires,
Needs, and wants,
Fills another ditch.

The holy books
Will rise again
And continue the cycle.

Easy

Adam and Eve
Were lazy.

Modern society
Will not forgive
The lassitude
Of loafing.

Create,
Don't think
Of oblivion.

Distractions

Toys maintain
Our continuing childhood.

Why discontinue
Our sense of wonderment
That leads us
Down the path
To ultimate,
Dazzling,
Heavenly glory.

Paradise
Has unknown toys.

Postponed

When
Will the true tomorrow
Arrive?

Plans are like an accordion,
They expand
Only to contract.

I must believe
That tomorrow
Is the day
Of the solution.

Revisited

Try to keep it like that,
My memory fails.

As we move ahead
Into the future,
Old haunts
And old sights
Hopefully will retain
Their charm.

Yeah, I was there.

Sure

Of course,
I've been there.

I visited Rome
At an Italian restaurant;
Just as I gazed
At the Grand Canal
Of Venice
While looking along
A drainage ditch.

It's a matter
Of detail.

Firing

Small boys
Still love guns.

Word change
But not
Our basic drives.

Men still want
To reach
For the illusory.

Expanding

Virtue led
To nothingness.

Sam was very rich
Yet he left it all
To enter
A monastery.

Some are satisfied
With losing it all.

Herd

He lost himself
In numbers.

Everyman
Runs with the crowd;
Screaming and banner waving,
And raising a lot of dust.

We readily
Stomped them.

Sun

Sunrise fortune
Will rise up.

There are still
Scouts
That enjoy
Showing the way
Through the pass.

A firm hand
Is a railroad track.

Question

He owned
A lot of
Plaques and medals.

A tombstone
Is the pelt
Of his life.

It all meant nothing
To other eyes.

Continual

Don't wake up
The babies.

Small boys
Are run out
So that the infants
May enjoy
Their rest.

The ramifications
Will increase.

Stop

I'll quit
Next year.

Many a little girl
May say,
"This is the last game
I'll play."

Promises disappear
Like drops
In the water of a pool.

Unchanging

Some things still remain
The same.

Men still prefer
Women
When it's time
To eat.

He learned to prepare
Many dishes.

Afraid

They retired
To their castle.

Who else
Might be living
In one
Of the many rooms.

Old folks
Lose track.

Mounds

Uneasiness rises
With cabin fever.

Who would spend
So much time
Creating
A cathedral?

A restrictive society
Loves monuments.

End

My life will run
To how many pages?

After an existence
Of doubts
Like walking on ice
With patent leather shoes,
I have to remark
That it hasn't been easy.

Closing the ledger
Left some loose ends.

0-595-33702-3

Lightning Source UK Ltd.
Milton Keynes UK

173609UK00001B/102/A